# OUT OF THE DARKNESS

## POEMS ABOUT FINDING STRENGTH, HOPE, AND LOVE

ZACK RIPLEY

For questions, comments, concerns, address the publisher at smalltownpoetry@aol.com

For ordering information please contact publisher at email listed above

First edition

# INTRODUCTION

The book you are about to read is a collection of poems I have written over the past five years. As the title suggests, the poems are about finding strength, hope, and love.

For your convenience, these poems are organized alphabetically and categorized by theme.

WARNING: some of these poems talk about potentially sensitive topics, including domestic violence, suicidal thoughts, and drug addiction. These poems are meant to offer a different perspective on these situations and offer hope and encouragement to escape them. Resources are available in the back of the book.

Thank you for your support. I hope these poems inspire you and help you get through whatever you are struggling with.

Two dollars from the sale of every book will be donated to The Jed Foundation, who partner with high schools and colleges to educate about teen suicide, drug abuse, and protect the mental health of teens and young adults. You can find out more about them at jedfoundation.org

ACKNOWLEDGMENTS

So many people to thank! First, thank mom and dad of course. Thank you for believing in me and helping me finance this book.

Thank you Ciec, Karen, Mary Ann and Dave, Nick, Courtney, Mary Jo, and so many more for your unwavering support and belief in my gifts.

Thank you to Pat from Turbo Taxi for giving me a second and third poem journal.

Thank you to Michael Amidei and the World Poetry Open Mic community.

Thank you, Frank, for making me think about how the poems should flow.

Thank you, Mrs. Countryman and Mr. Martin, for making me love English and helping me get through high school.

And, finally, I need to thank you Kelly. There is no way this book would be possible if you hadn't pushed me and inspired me to follow my passion.

Table of Contents

# STRENGTH

The following poems are meant to show you that whatever doubts or insecurities you have about yourself or who you are as a person, there's a way to overcome them. You are stronger than you know or give yourself credit for.

## Ask (it's okay)

You tell yourself lies to get through the day
Because you feel like no one will believe what you say.
No one understands how cruel they can be to you.
They tell you they love you, and that's all it takes
To forgive them until the next time they break.
Deep in your heart, you know that's not what love really is.
Take it from someone on the outside looking in.
They're starting to do damage to more than just your skin.
If you don't get out now, I fear it's only a matter of time
Before you become a victim of the most heinous crime.
It's okay to ask for help.
It's okay for any of us to.
It may not seem fair to tell people about our struggles.
It may not seem right.
But if you let someone help,
Eventually, they will help you find your light.

## Doubts

They're swinging left and swinging right.
They hide in the shadows just out of sight.
But how can I fight what I cannot see?
How can I stop them from breaking every piece of me?
If you're out there and feeling all alone,
You don't have to fight all on your own.
Because the more you ask for help,
The more you take control.
And when you take control and feel it in your soul,
The doubts will start to disappear.
Doubts: the bullies of the mind.
Doubts: leave no trace of them behind.
Now that you know how to fight back,
It's time to put it to the test.
Take it one step, one day at a time,
And we'll figure out the rest.

## I control my wonderful world of color

Today, the sky was sunny and bright.
Like ice cream, cold but light.
Then, the sky turned gray
As the wind and snow welcomed the night.
I look up, down and around,
And wish I didn't feel so helpless here on the ground.
I can't control the weather. This is true.
But there are things I can control and so can you.
We can control what we learn.
We control what we type.
We control whether we run or stand up and fight.
We control all these things and so much more.
But you never know what life has in store.
One more thing to think about.
If we could control everything,
Life would be so much duller.
Maybe that's why my favorite thing I control
Is how much of the world I see in color.

## It’s okay

It's okay to find shapes in the clouds
Or stand out in the crowd.
It's okay to ask why
Or if you feel you need to cry.
It's okay to say no.
It's okay if you don't know.
It's okay if your dreams change as you grow.
It's okay if you're wrong.
It's okay if you're right.
It's okay to ask for help or if you're afraid of the night.
It's okay to sing.
It's okay to love who you love.
It's okay to believe in heaven and your god above.
It's okay if you're lonely.
It's okay to admit you're not okay.
But remember.
No matter what they say, it's okay.

## Life is a boat on the sea

Doc tells me I’m still alive.
Don't know how;
But not complaining.
Just trying to live in the here and now.
But that doesn't mean I've forgotten my past.
Think about life as a boat on the open sea.
The mast, the pole in the center of the boat, is your past.
It's the foundation and holds up the sail,
Which is your future.
You're the captain. The one who controls the here and now.
Your loved ones are your power.
The wind that pushes you forward.
And the sea, that's the most important part.
It represents the unknown.
The things you can't control.
There will be days when the thunder claps
And your boat floods from whitecaps.
I know it's hard,
But if you don't worry about what you can't control,
And don't block out your past,
You can give your all to someone
And find happiness that lasts.

## Out of the darkness into the light

Years ago, I was a teen.
I was afraid to make friends
Because kids were mean.
So, one day, I decided to wander around my mind
To see if there was any strength I could find.
I thought if I could be strong,
It wouldn't hurt when they called me fat and stupid.
That once they realized it didn't affect me anymore,
They would get bored and move along.
I thought I knew where I needed to go, but got lost.
I found myself somewhere I didn't know.
Finally, I found a door.
And when I rushed through,
All I saw was darkness. Nothing more.
I tried to find my way back.
But after a while,
I made myself so scared,
I got dizzy and fell.
Then everything went black.
When I came to,
I realized trying to ignore my feelings
Wouldn't make me strong.
That it wasn't my job to prove they were wrong.
There in the darkness, I realized I was strong all along.
When I believed in myself,
I got back my sight.
It felt like a lifetime,
But I finally found my way
Out of the darkness and into the light.

# Pride

There's this feeling inside.
It's something I've never experienced before.
But suddenly, I feel so alive.
I looked it up and it's called pride.
It all started the night you left.
I got a phone call from one of your friends.
When I hung up, I knew it was the beginning of the end.
You told me you loved me.
And when I realized you lied,
I crawled into bed as I screamed, then cried.
After I let go of the anger and the pain,
It was like the sun came out and dried up all the rain.
I found the strength to let you go.
It's okay if you feel bad,
But I want to thank you.
You taught me I'm stronger than I know.

## Pursuit of Happiness

It's a big mistake
Staring at the ticking clock.
Waiting for an opportunity to knock.
Nothing's going to fall at your door.
So, find something worth fighting for.
When you realize success in life
Is not defined by your wealth,
You can begin on a journey toward the pursuit of happiness
That will ultimately better your health.
On this journey,
There may be times when your heart may break.
And the pain may feel like it's too much to take.
But if you can find the strength to carry on,
You'll find the things you do
Will be remembered long after you're gone.

## You deserve more

If you don't think I'm trying,
You're wrong.
At first, I was just trying to find somewhere I belong.
But somewhere along the way,
I realized I wanted something more.
I deserved something more.
Sometimes, we forget what's worth fighting for.
We forget who we are.
We forget it's okay to reach for the stars.
Sometimes, people need to remember
That just because they can't see them,
It doesn't mean we don't have scars.
But the truth is,
Everyone has scars in some way, shape, or form.
Proof that at one point,
They were able to ride out a storm.
Everyone's journey is different,
But there are two things I know for sure.
We're all human,
And you deserve more.

## You don’t have to

You don’t have to wish you could be strong.
It takes courage to stay alive
When you feel trapped and in pain.
You didn’t know it,
But you’ve been strong all along.
You don’t have to wish you could feel
Like you had somewhere to belong.
You’re human.
You’re in a club bigger than you could ever imagine.
So, go ahead.
Sing your song.
You don’t have to be afraid you aren’t enough.
The fact that you’re standing here
Proves you can push through
When the going gets rough.
Bottom line,
You don’t have to think, wish, or be afraid of anything.
Because you already are everything.

## Your Power

Where there is darkness, there is light.
Where there is wrong, there is right.
But where is it tonight?
Is it in the alley down the street?
Or is it right beneath our feet?
The truth is, it's with you.
You can call upon this power
When you feel you are about to meet
Your darkest and loneliest hours.
Whatever way it takes form,
Be it a friend, movie, or song,
If you let it, it will help you weather any storm.
Happiness can be achieved by all
When we find the courage to break down our walls.
It may make you vulnerable, but that's okay.
Believe in your power,
And you will live to find another day.

# HOPE

Pretty self-explanatory. But the most important thing to have in anything, be it a relationship, a job, addiction, or just life in general, is hope. Hopefully these poems inspire you to have hope.

## Balance

Gray skies.
No sun.
All work,
No fun.
That's not okay.
If you have passions,
And your parents say,
"Don't waste your time.
You'll never make a living that way."
Please don't walk away.
Because in a world
Of so much stress, and so much fear,
Balance is crucial to your health.
Even more so the closer you get to your older years.
And when you have doubts,
When you feel like no one believes in you,
And you don't even believe in yourself,
Know that I believe in you.
I truly do.

## Don’t give up on love

Every day, you feel like you're dying inside.
Trying to ignore the pain
Gifted by a world that can be so unkind.
You look in the mirror and try to like what you see.
But the ones who broke your heart
Won't let you see how beautiful you are.
If you feel alone, scared to trust the ones that love you
Because you feel like they won't understand,
It's easy to push love away
When you feel like you're the only one
Who knows your heart,
And you're the only one who can.
But please, don't give up on love.
Don't give up on your heart.
Forget about the ones
Who couldn't see your beautiful soul right from the start.
Don't give up on your dreams
And someday you'll find
This crazy life can be so much better than it seems.
So, please, don't give up on love.

## Have you ever?

Have you ever been confused about how you feel
Because you're not sure what's real?
Have you ever been filled with dread
Because you can't get out of your head?
I have too.
Have you ever been picked on in school
And done something desperate
Just to make them think you're cool?
Have you ever neglected yourself
By pushing your feelings aside
Because you were afraid of what would happen
If they found out how much you were hurting inside?
I have too.
What I'm trying to say
Is that if you feel like you're alone, you're not.
Take it from me. If you can find the courage
To ask to talk to someone, it can help a lot.

## It’s going to be alright

I want to tell you that it’s going to be alright.
I want to tell you whatever I have to
To get you through the night.
I want to tell you how proud I am
That you asked for help as I hold you tight.
No matter how much you scream and cry and shake,
I won’t give up the fight.
I want to tell you that it’s not your fault.
And as we sit by the fire,
Watching it fill the room with warmth and light,
I want to tell you it’s going to be alright.

## Just because

Just because it's called makeup
Doesn't mean it has to make up who you are.
Just because someone is bullying you
Doesn't mean they're not being bullied too.
Just because someone tells you
You're stupid or ugly, doesn't mean it's true.
Now, it's true that just because you read something,
It doesn't make it true.
But it's important to know
That just because you're feeling blue,
It doesn't mean it's the end of happiness for you.

### Lost. Ready to be found.

It’s scary being lost.
Feeling lost. Alone.
So cold, you can feel it in your bones.
But the thing about being lost,
You can always be found.
Found by a person. By faith.
You can even find yourself.
If you’re out there,
And you want to be found,
If you’re READY to be found,
Call out your name.
Someone who can help
Will listen for the sound.

## More like a river, less like a wall

Another day here.
Another day gone.
Another day wishing I had somewhere I belonged.
Another day comes.
Another day goes.
Another new day with nothing to show.
Another day begins.
Another day ends.
Another day with no new friends.
But in spite of it all,
I still hold on to hope
That someday, someone will help me
Be more like a river
And less like a wall.

## Sometimes

Sometimes, you're going to make mistakes.
Sometimes, you're going to say the wrong thing.
But in time, you'll learn
That doesn't mean you've done something wrong.
Sometimes, you're going to crash and burn.
But sometimes, that's the only way we learn.
Now that you've lived and learned, you can move on.
So, don't be afraid when you fall.
Go ahead, break down your walls.
You're going to see beauty you never knew was there before.
Go on, hold your head high.
Jump up. Reach for the sky.
And remember.
Sometimes, there will be days nothing turns out right.
But someday, everything will be alright.

## Talking will set you free

You be my Bonnie,
I'll be your Clyde.
Together, we'll take this life for one hell of a ride.
You be my Thelma,
I'll be your Louise.
We'll get in the car and do whatever we damn well please.
Life on the run with the one you love may sound fun.
But no matter how far or how fast you go,
Eventually, you will always fly too close to the sun.
It doesn't matter if you run from pain or fear.
Your mind is like an elephant.
It never really forgets,
So, your problems will always reappear.
What you choose to do is up to you.
But take it from me.
Talking about your pain will set you free.

## Who are you?

If you don’t know, I can’t tell you who you are.
I can’t tell you what you’ll be.
But I can tell you what I see.
When I look in your eyes,
I see pain you’ve been trying to disguise.
I see you hoping you can find hope.
And when I look at your face,
I see someone who could never be replaced.
I can see you feel a hundred years older
Because you’ve been carrying
The weight of the world on your shoulders.
Watching your chest move
When you put your hand on your heart,
That’s proof you’re human.
And if you want to know who you are,
That’s a good place to start.
But in the end, it doesn’t matter what I see.
All that matters is you find a way to love who you are
And look forward to who you’ll be.

# LOVE

Love is literally what gives us life most of the time. Yes, it’s important that we feel love from other people. But I have come to find the saying is true. It is a lot easier for someone else to love you if you find a way to love yourself. And you don’t have to love everything about yourself. Even if you find just one thing you love about who you are as a person or the way you present yourself to people, it can be incredibly rewarding and give you a higher level of confidence. These poems are about finding love in different ways. Loving yourself, feeling love for others, people loving you, even caring about you is a form of love.

## Because of you

You say I'm beautiful.
Well, baby, if that's true, I'm only beautiful because of you.
I wish you could understand how special you make me feel.
And I am proud to make it my purpose
To make you believe that your beauty is real.
Every day, you give me a reason to live.
And now it's my turn to give you all I have to give.
I can't wait to thank you for all you've given me so far.
Because of you, I am proud of who we are.

## I love being your mirror

"Mirror, mirror, on the wall"
Is what I hear you say.
Yes, I am the mirror on the wall.
What can I do for you today?
We've been together so long,
What can I show you that you haven't seen before?
I've shown you your beautiful, strong hair.
The cute freckles on your cheeks.
The light in your hazel eyes,
And your lips that make men weak.
I've shown you with your makeup.
I've shown you your smile when you let your hair down.
It hurt to show you your tears when he broke your heart,
But I was so proud to show you in your wedding gown.
I know it may seem strange coming from a mirror,
But seeing gray in your hair, I can't help but stop and stare.
Looking back,
I think the best part of being a part of your show
Is seeing how much confidence
You've gained as you've grown.
Before our time comes to an end,
There are two things I hope you know are true.
I love being your mirror,
And I will only ever have eyes for you.

## I love you. Please stay.

Every day, I worked that nine to five.
Pot of coffee every morning made me feel alive.
But by the end of the day,
After dinner with the wife and kid,
The demons I kept away came back.
So, I had a date with Jack until the world went black.
For years, I suffered in silence.
I eventually turned to drugs
To try and escape the violence gifted by the tyrants.
But no matter how many times
I pushed the trigger and pulled the thread,
Every time I came down,
I couldn't help but feel I was better off dead.
Just when I was ready to quit,
That's when I met her.
That was it.
I finally found someone who cared.
We got married, and our son was born.
I had never been more scared.
But we survived.
We pushed through.
Life was perfect until the fight we had when he was two.
We said some things we didn't mean,
And I walked away again never to be seen.
I'm telling you this because it's too late for me.
But it's not too late for you.
If you feel like you're ready to face the end,
Please let me say what I needed someone to say.
I love you. Please stay.

## In your honor

I breathe in and out
Trying to clear my head
Of all the things I thought about
But never actually said.
Even though I never got a chance to tell you
You meant the world to me,
I know you knew it; it was plain to see.
You took so much of me when you left,
I still don’t know what to do.
But in your honor,
I will keep on pushing through.
I know someday you'll show me the way.
But, for now, you're in my heart
And that's where you'll stay.

## I remember

So many things I’ve said.
So much I have left to say.
But I don’t think I have enough time
To find the words that keep getting lost along the way.
Don’t be afraid if I forget who I am today,
Because I still remember who we were yesterday.
I remember the nights by the fire with a bottle of wine.
I remember the day you said you’d be mine.
I remember all the years we were young, wild, free.
I remember all the dreams we had
About how great our kids’ future would be.
I remember the love. I remember the fights.
I remember the summers on the island
Watching the fireworks light up the night.
Even if it doesn’t show,
There’s one thing I need you to know.
I remember.

## The same

If I had a million dollars,
Or not even a dime to my name,
As long as I'm with you, it's all the same.
It doesn't matter if we lived in a mansion
or a cardboard box.
As long as I'm with you,
It's all the same.
On our wedding day,
I can't promise I won't cry
As your father walks you down the aisle
And you leave his arm for mine.
If, down the road,
You decide I can't make you happy anymore,
I will let you leave even though it will break me at the core.
Don't worry. I won't try to win you back.
You gave me a lifetime of happiness,
And that's all I can ask.
I got through the days before I met you,
So, I know I can do it again.
But if you ask me to rate my happiness, it won't be a ten.
Life is the name of the game.
And once you find the one you love,
It will never be the same.

## Truth about love

I told you once. I told you twice.
If I have to tell you again, I'm going to stop being nice.
It doesn't matter if you're black or white.
Gay or straight.
The longer you live,
The more you realize love doesn't discriminate.
And when this truth becomes real,
So does the truth that you are worthy of love,
And your heart can heal.

## You make me ready for more

I need to get something off my chest.
When it comes to friends, there's no second best.
And when it comes to people I love,
Every time I look at you, I forget about the rest.
It's amazing how your words give me so much hope.
Like a street lamp guiding me home in the night.
And yet, when I finally find the words I want to say,
I look at you and it's like I'm being hit with kryptonite.
I don't know what the future has in store.
But as long as you're in my life,
You make me ready for more.

## You make me smile

How can I show you I care
About more than just your looks
Or the clothes that you wear?
How can I make you understand
That all I need to be happy is to hold your hand?
I know guys hurt you in the past.
And it doesn't mean much when we say we're different.
That we're going to last.
So, I won't say any of that.
I'll just keep on loving you until you love me too.
Even if that never happens,
There's one thing I need to make sure is clear.
Every day I spend with you makes me smile ear to ear.

## Beautiful Voices

This poem doesn’t fall under any of the categories in the title, but it had an important message and I didn’t want to leave it out. It’s called Beautiful Voices.

It was a dark and stormy night
When an angel of death took flight.
She took to the skies and followed the thunder
To the one who would begin their eternal slumber.
The man who would soon receive such a fate
Denied the love of someone great.
He told her she was ugly
And didn't have time
To give his love to someone who wasn't divine.
Then, what happened next,
Devastated her parents when they read her text.
He had no remorse when he was given the news.
So, the angel of death made him pay his dues.
People take things for granted.
That's to be expected.
But professing love is not an act
That deserves being disrespected.
If we took the time to think about
All of the outcomes of our choices,
The world might not lose so many beautiful voices.

## Resources

These days, shining a light in the darkness is harder than it sounds. But don't give up. There are still people looking to be found. If you're looking to be found, or if you need help, please visit these resources.

### Domestic Violence

This is a link to the national domestic violence hot line. It offers anonymous chat and call in but this page in particular also lists organizations by state if you want more local help. There are also links on the page to organizations that specialize in violence between teens and the lgbtq community. https://www.thehotline.org/resources/victims-and-survivors/

### Drug and alcohol abuse

This is a link to an organization that offers resources and facts about not only drug abuse, but also for children whose parents struggle with alcohol addiction, people who have suicidal thoughts, and people with eating disorders. It has an anonymous text line, an anonymous phone line, and links to get help in specific states.
https://abovetheinfluence.com/resources/

### Suicide prevention

This link is to the resource page for the American foundation for suicide prevention. It offers resources to anonymous text and call hot lines for not only suicide, but everything associated with mental health including eating disorders, depression, and anxiety.
https://afsp.org/find-support/resources/

Made in the USA
Columbia, SC
21 April 2025